Revealing the Untold Truth

The Second Generation

———————

Efraim "Effy" Eckhaus

Revealing the Untold Truth: The Second Generation
Copyright © 2010-2011

Dedication

To my father:

In loving memory of my late father Moneik Michal, for instilling his courage, values, and wisdom in me while I was growing up. With out him I wouldn't be the man I am today. I am forever grateful. Thank you dad, I miss you!

To my mother:

To my dear mother Nina, you have been the universal bond that has held this family together during the toughest of times, and for that I thank you. You are truly the greatest example of what perseverance is and always will be. I love you!

To my wife:

In appreciation of my beloved wife Michelle Eckhaus, over the years your love, support, and devotion have made everything possible. I love you!

To my daughter:

To my beautiful daughter Jennifer, you have brought me the most joy and given me the greatest grandchildren. What more could a father ask for. I love you!

Table of Contents

Introduction

When my mother began to open up and tell me about her life during WWII, I was glad that I took the time to sit with her and learn more about how she was once forced to live her life. After listening to many stories, I was truly amazed at how very little I actually knew about someone that I was so close to my whole life.

Some of the first stories I remembered hearing were those of my mother being forced to work in Poland as a slave laborer. As she continued on about her hardships, I started to realize that I was about to inherit a lifelong weight to carry on my shoulders, which was the legacy of being a second-generation survivor.

Over the years, parents that lived through the Holocaust passed their stories along to second-generation children, which have greatly impacted their lives as they themselves passed through adulthood, parenthood, and now for me, middle age. For many years Jewish parents worked diligently to ensure that their children would never forget the atrocities committed during the Holocaust. To this day, these stories have had the greatest of impact on each and everyone's lives. The second-generation children know that their family's legacy has been passed down to them.

There were daily reminders of what our parents were made to suffer through against their will. During the Eichmann trials, I can vividly remember feeling that it was our obligation to watch and learn of the unthinkable crimes that took place during the Holocaust. Watching the trials made us feel helpless and very sad just knowing that we were unable to be there to protect our parents. It was not uncommon for survivors to have disturbing memories emerge throughout their lives. Many parents were visited regularly by nightmares each and every night, and their children shared the pain by experiencing these episodes first hand.

Knowing what their parents went through made the children at times feel almost as unwelcome as their parents once were. Growing up, many of us felt as if they lived through and labored in their own "personal" concentration camp, right in their very own home.

There was a constant feeling of frustration in homes due to the fact that Holocaust survivors were so overly protective of their children. We were also very protective of our parents, and felt guilty when they found out that we were looking out for them. If you were a parent and your child thought that they had to protect you, you would feel much too vulnerable.

I can remember feeling a bit embarrassed when I knew I was being too over protective of my mother. I did not want her to think for a minute that I felt she was unable to take care of herself, but the stories I heard affected me so much that I was concerned about what could happen to her at any time. My mother would point out that issues we would disagree about were nothing compared to what her and my father had gone through during the Holocaust.

Many Holocaust survivors lived within a code of silence outside of their homes because they did not want people to know what they had gone through. It also became increasingly difficult for the second-generation to communicate the problems in their lives to their parents as nothing could quite compare to what they had dealt with. The code of silence would eventually become bilateral for many of us. I was now painfully aware of the past suffering of my parents and felt ashamed that I may have not considered my mother's feelings when bringing up my own issues or concerns.

Even though it was hard to manage, survivors were compelled to live as normal a life as possible. Our parents were living with terrible memories that no human being should ever endure. While everyone around Holocaust survivors had their own individual identity, we were all caught up in the distress of the matter. That's the one thing I can attest to above all else, is just how close we were brought together through the pain and suffering.

Despite my family's psychological scars, we lead productive lives of hope, renewal, and success. Even today, the evil from mid-twentieth century still continues in a world where racial prejudice and anti-semitism are still an everyday threat. We all live with the remembrance of what our loved ones went through and are proud to be the second-generation survivors.

The Story Of My Father

I want to take the opportunity to personally walk you through brief stages of my father's life. This chapter will encompass his years as a young boy happily farming his parent's land, only to lose his parents and face the pressures of living in an orphanage. He would later leave his country and escape to the safety of Russia. As a young man he would learn of family members being taken during the invasion and of their subsequent deportations from Wlodawa to their untimely deaths in concentration camps.

My father would prove to be honorable and display the character necessary to carry out the most unselfish act one could commit, volunteering to fight in the war and help liberate his birth country.

My dad was born on September 7, 1922 in Woldawa Poland Mordechai Motel Eckhaus, the son of Polish Jewish parents. His family owned a large farm, which they raised cattle and other farm animals. They also bred Horses for the Polish military. When he was old enough, my father would work side by side with his family in the fields all the while keeping up with his school studies and chores around the house.

My father was raised in a household that was religious, conservative, and nationalistic. It was these values that helped in developing his upbringing and molded his character early on. He would attend religious school that was styled in the form of a Cheder (Hebrew School).

Unfortunately, my father would lose his mother (my grandmother) at an early age due to illness, but my dad kept up with the farming and continued on with his schooling until a few years later when his father (my grandfather) passed away. Once my father and his siblings had lost both parents, they were sent to live and learn in an orphanage.

Shortly thereafter, the neighboring country of Germany would invade Poland unannounced. You could see and hear the German soldiers crossing the bridge over the river. The Nazis ultimately had taken over the bridge and made their way in to Wlodawa. Once in Wlodawa, the Germans spared no time and started unmercifully shooting civilians. The sound of the military tanks rumbling in to town was thunderous. The Germans began firing in the direction of buildings and any other structure they felt stood in their way. The scene was of frenzied proportions. The dead littered the streets and the dying lay there bleeding unable to help themselves. Even if anyone could help them it was too dangerous as the living were frantically trying to find cover from the gunfire. In the wake of assault, there was nothing but death and destruction all around us.

Once the assault ended and the smoke had cleared, the Nazis began to carry out orders for citizens to come out of their homes or be subjected to removal by force. The town's people stood there confused as to what they were witnessing. Standing there with only the clothes on their backs, the Nazis began to beat, torture, and kill innocent people without cause or provocation. There was mass chaos and confusion as to what they were to do and just what was to become of everyone. The Nazis organized the people into groups and marched them to the town square. In the square there was much uncertainty as the Nazis began to "sort" people into groups. As families were being separated from loved ones, they continued to beat people regardless of what they may or may not have done. This was truly a tumultuous time.

After the initial invasion, an aunt made them aware that they too had to be in the town square with the others. It was at that point that they were forced to live in the newly formed ghetto along with a lot of the families from their hometown. It was there that my father, along with his younger brother's and sister's, realized that they would live, work, and suffer together without the protection and guidance of their parents. There were few relatives in the ghetto with them.

They may still have been alone, but one major difference is that they were no longer in the confinements and structure of the orphanage. Now more than ever they had to rely on one another and take the lessons that they had learned from their parents growing up as well as the disciplines they developed working on the farm and use it to their advantage.

It was also in that instant he knew he would have to care for himself and his younger siblings. Even at his young age, my father was aware of his surroundings and knew that he must act quickly in order to keep everyone safe and maintain their health to some degree. Showing no fear, at night my father would sneak out of the ghetto in search of food to care for his family. He would go to local farms or anywhere else he felt he could gather food and cautiously smuggle it back into the ghetto without being detected. It was the only way he knew how to provide for his brother's and sister's.

Many did not survive as the conditions were deplorable and food was scarce. People were dying from malnutrition due to starvation because they were much to weak to fend for themselves. He was insistent that he was not going to let that happen to his siblings while living in the ghetto!

After witnessing his uncle die in the ghetto at the hands of the Nazis, that same evening, my father decided it was much too dangerous to continue on in the ghetto. My father approached his older brother Efraim and asked if he could help the younger siblings escape with him to Russia; Efraim said it was too risky and decided against taking the kids. One day the Germans would come into the ghetto and called for the deportation of children, the old, and anyone unfit to work. These poor souls were the first to be sent to Sobibor extermination camp and murdered. Knowing that his family was rounded up and taken to perish, motivated my father that much more to leave the ghetto. He had the foresight to see that it was only a matter of time before he would be sent to a concentration camp or worse.

My father determined that it was time to make a decision. The decision was made to escape to the forest and take his chances outside the unforgiving brick walls of hell. Escaping from the ghetto was no easy task! It required traveling through areas that were busy with Nazi policemen as well as civilian collaborators who could spot escaping Jews quickly and alert the Nazis. Hiding by day and moving by night proved difficult, but that tactic was the only way my father could get around without being detected.

At night the sounds of sirens broke the silence while floodlights swirled around illuminating the darkness detecting the slightest movements. During the day, the Nazi police would patrol the streets with their weapons and guard dogs so; hiding was the best alternative during the day and taking chances on foot at night proved to be the better option.

Luckily, my father made it through the city streets. As he found his way in to the forest on the Polish/Russian boarder, he met up with Jewish Resistance Partisans. The Partisans would take the time to teach my father the necessary warfare and tactics he would need in order to assist and survive the resistance. Like my father, thousands of Jews escaped the ghettos and joined the Partisan units. At that time as many as 10,000 Jews survived the war by taking refuge in the forest with the Jewish Partisans fighting units. In some of the Partisan camps they established "family" camps in which Jewish civilians would repair weapons, made clothing, and cooked for the fighters. My father would assist in a number of missions with the Partisans, which would later help him prepare for the fight of his life.

After leaving the woods and the Partisans behind, my father found work for a short time in a large factory to help support himself all the while continuing to search for his older brother Efraim. From time to time my father would sneak over the boarder back into Poland in hopes that he could seek out and possibly locate missing family members. Unfortunately he did not have any luck finding anyone.

As he befriended a few select people he began to hear stories about independent Polish army units forming to help the Russians fight against the Germans. My father was a young man when he gave everything of himself for his family and country. He unequivocally decided to do the admirable thing and enlisted to fight with the Polish army units in Russia against the machine that was Hitler's military. It was Hitler's and the Nazis plan to ethnically cleanse the Jewish race and began to systematically exterminate all Jews of Europe, which resulted in the deaths of approximately six million Jews.

My father in his own words carefully told the stories of surviving the Holocaust. He also told stories of the combat scenarios he took part in as well as the pain he endured getting wounded in battle, which he received a number of medals for courage under fire. I would also learn that it was difficult for my father to teach me of my heritage as my father didn't have any photographs and hardly mentioned his family or the family's past, only of what he could slightly remember from time to time. Be it told, most survivors deeply suppressed painful memories inadvertently in order to try to live as normal lives as possible. As years passed, memories would sometime surface and they would relive the torment over again and again within their minds

By telling his stories about the Holocaust, escaping to Russia, and the war helped to write and document our memoirs. This process forces us to recall the painful memories, but also helps us to considerately bring to mind their emotional and physical triumphs that survivor's may very well have buried deep beneath the scars of hurt they suffered at the hands of a tyrannical dictator.

Persecution of Jews

Out of all the religious groups in the world, none have suffered as much as the Jews. Jewish people have been exiled from almost every country that they have ever lived in, starting with Israel, and most recently ending with many countries across Europe.

The Jews have not only been exiled from many countries, but had been tortured and murdered while living in them. The Jews have proven to be a very strong people from surviving thousands of years by bringing their religion with them from one country to the next, while never loosing their faith in god, their people, or their religion.

Thousands of years ago, Jews lived in Jerusalem until King Nebuchadnezzer had conquered the city and forced them into exile in the city of Babylon.

After seventy years of exile, the Jews were allowed to return to Jerusalem, although most decided to stay in Babylon. The Jews that stayed became merchants, traders, and bankers. The Jewish people prospered due to extended trade routes that existed throughout the region.

The Jews lived in peace for a few hundred years after they were first exiled to Babylon. The Jews would begin to be persecuted, murdered, and expelled when the crusades descended on the Jews in Europe.

The first acts of true anti-semitism in Europe were committed by Christians armed with the belief that the Jews had killed Jesus, and therefore deserved to suffer for all eternity. These Christians believed that all Jewish people were guilty of persecuting Jesus as highlighted in the bible during his crucifixion. Christians came together to unofficially charge the Jews with "Deicide" (God Killing). For most of the existence of Christianity this thinking has led to the hatred and murder of innocent Jews. Although in the Middle Ages the "Deicide" was a major reason for the persecution of the Jews, this is just one of many uncountable blames placed on them.

During the first Crusade (which some consider to be the very first Holocaust) Jewish communities in Europe were attacked and completely destroyed. Many crusaders did not know why they should travel thousands of miles to the Holy Land to convert non-believers when there were already non-believers in their own countries that needed converting. Many Jews were slaughtered and others were forcefully made to convert against their will. Some wealthy Jews paid off attackers in order to be spared. Throughout the multiple crusades thereafter, Jews were always in constant and present danger.

After suffering through the Crusades, the remaining Jews began to be expelled from many European countries. They were banished from England, France, and Austria.

When the Black Plague fell upon Europe, the Jews were blamed for poisoning wells. During this time, if a child went missing, they would be accused of using the missing child's blood for Jewish rituals.

In Spain, during the Granada massacre, more then 1,500 Jewish families (totaling an estimated 4,000 people) were murdered in a single day. This unprovoked treatment was a regular occurrence as populations in many countries across Europe chose to use the Jewish communities as their scapegoat for each and every problem they faced.

In the Papal States (which later would become sections of Italy) Jews were required to live only in specified neighborhoods called ghettos. They were also required to attend church, and were constantly urged to become Christians. There was a special tax that only Jews would have to pay, which financed the Jewish converts study of Christianity. There were many instances of forced baptism. After these baptisms, the State would separate the people who were involuntarily baptized from their families.

Jews of the world did not just suffer from the Christians hands. Muhammad himself, the founder of Islam, had beheaded all men and pubescent boys from the largest Jewish tribe in Medina that refused to convert to Islam, and then took their women and children as slaves (also taking a beautiful newly widowed woman for himself).

Traditionally, Jews living in Muslim lands were allowed to practice their own religion, but were treated very unequally. There were many massacres of the Jewish people in Muslim lands, as well as forced conversions.

The Muslim population in Baghdad would mock the Jews, and beat them in the streets. Jews were forced to pay a tax for being a free adult non-Muslim male to the Muslims. The Jews suffered from many social and legal problems such as being unable to bear arms, and were not permitted to give testimony in a court of law with cases regarding Muslims.

Jewish women were required to wear one black and one red shoe with a small brass bell attached to each shoe (or around their neck). When the bell sounded, it would alert everyone that a Jewish woman was around him or her. Jewish men were required to wear a yellow badge on their headgear and a neckpiece made of lead inscribed with the word "dhimmi" to show that they had to pay a poll tax.

Dhimmi is a word used to describe a non-muslim who is forced to live as a second-class citizen because they are living in an area ruled by Muslims. Dhimmi's must accept a restrictive and humiliating existence to the supposedly "superior" Muslims, to avoid enslavement or death. Aside from the restrictions and humiliation Dhimmi's were subjected to, they must also pay a special tax to Muslims as a tribute.

There was no end to the suffering of the Jewish people. Even after death Jews could suffer monetarily if they had left any debt behind. It did not matter if the debt was a very small or large amount. When a Jew died in debt, Muslims forced the Jewish community to cover the debt of the deceased, or they would unceremoniously burn the body instead of traditionally burying it.

Throughout the world, and all throughout time, the Jews would be blamed for everyone's problems and misfortunes. Jewish communities would always face constant massacres, but nothing in history would amount to what was going to happen during the reign of the Nazis, the Third Reich of Germany. The Nazis would create an empire that was going to make it a priority to rid Europe of all Jews by unmatchable large-scale mass-murder.

Nazis

The Holocaust is generally regarded as the "systematic, state-sponsored persecution and slaughter of approximately six million Jews" that occurred during the reign of the Nazis in Europe.

While the Jews became the main target during the Holocaust, there were many other groups that suffered. These groups included Poles, Czechs, Greeks, Gypsies, Serbs, Ukrainians, and Russians, as well as homosexuals, trade unionists, Prisoners of War, and Jehovah's Witnesses. Mentally and physically handicapped persons were subjected to the euthanasia program, which was specifically designed to exterminate them along with children and the old. In the Nazis disillusioned minds, they felt that the euthanasia program was the most humane and cost effective way to eliminate them. Each one of these groups was targeted because Germans believed they had racial inferiority.

Before the Nazis, anti-semitism in Germany became more public in the late 1800s, an influential historian named Heinrich von Trietschke published a collection of articles in which he wrote, "the Jews are our misfortune." The slogan would later be written on banners at Nazi rallies. Another German writer, Wilhelm Marr, coined the term "anti-semitism".

After WWI, Germany was in a terrible economic depression. Hitler made it easy for the German people to place the blame on the Jews while they were looking for answers to what went wrong with their country. Hitler told the German people that the Jews were to blame for Germany losing the war, and for the economy.

Hitler believed in racial purity and felt that German blood should remain as strong as possible, and that they must do away with other races.

In an early writing, Hitler stated, "rational anti-semitism must lead to a systematic legal opposition and elimination of the special privileges, which Jews hold... Its final objective must **unswervingly be the removal of the Jews altogether.**"

The Nazis became more and more popular as Hitler offered the German people solutions and promises to restore pride in Germany. By 1932, the Nazis were the largest political party in all Germany and soon had total control. Hitler called Germany the "Third Reich" because he felt it was going to be the third German Empire the world would have seen.

In 1933, Hitler had become chancellor of Germany and immediately began to attack anyone that was not part of his so-called master race. The media became controlled by the government censoring or removing anything against the Nazis. Newspapers, art, radio, and music became controlled by the Nazi regime.

Laws began to be put into action that took Jews out of public life. If you were a Jew you could not hold civil service jobs, or even university positions. Jewish businesses even became boycotted and a target for violence.

Eventually, all Jews were forced to wear a label on their clothing of a yellow Star of David with the word Juden (which translates to Jew).

Jews were also not allowed to go to public schools or theatres. They were also banned from walking in certain areas of Germany. By this time, the Jewish population of Europe was more than nine million strong (and a total of seventeen million strong worldwide).

The Nuremberg Race Laws were put in to effect in 1935. These laws made Jews unable to be a German citizen and made it illegal for Jews to marry Germans or have relationships with anyone who had "German or related blood".

The Nazis believed in not just keeping their blood pure, but also in advocating women to have as many German babies as possible. It was a German woman's job to stay at home and have children. The German government rewarded those families with large numbers of children; a special Mother's Cross was struck, given in bronze to German women who had four children, silver for six children, and gold for eight. Hundreds of thousands of these medals were given out to German mothers.

In 1933, a law was passed encouraging German couples to have babies through the Law for the Encouragement of Marriage. The Nazis had offered loans of 1,000 marks (the equivalent of nine months of work) to couples to get married. For each child the married couple had, ¼ of the loan did not have to be paid back, with the loan being paid off if the married couple had four children.

The Nazis believed if they were to make the German master race grow they needed more land for their people to prosper in. The Germans looked to their neighboring country Poland to expand.

The Nazis took Poland in 1939, and immediately began to put their plan in to action to make more room for Germans. One of the first steps was to kill all leaders and the intelligent. Professors, writers, politicians, and priests were hunted and murdered across Poland.

During the war, the Nazis created ghettos and forced the Jews to live in them under horrific conditions. There were over 400 ghettos, with the largest being Warsaw, where 450,000 Jews were crowded in to only 1.3 square miles. In Warsaw, thousands of Jews died every month from disease and starvation due to malnutrition.

Almost all ghettos were headed by a Judenrat, or governing Jewish council. This council was usually comprised of prominent leaders in the Jewish community, but was most often appointed by the Nazis, even in opposition to them, they were coerced to carry out the plans of the Third Reich in the ghetto for their people. The ghettos were human communities: there were both acts of avarice and nobility. Many tried to help one another stay alive under the harshest of circumstances.

Between 1933 and 1945, Nazi Germany established nearly 20,000 camps to imprison its millions of victims. These camps were used for a range of purposes including forced-labor camps, transit camps (which served as temporary way stations), and extermination camps built primarily or exclusively for mass murder. From its rise to power in 1933, the Nazi regime built a series of detention facilities to imprison and eliminate so-called enemies of the state. These facilities were called concentration camps because those imprisoned there were physically concentrated in one location.

To facilitate the Final Solution (the genocide or mass destruction of the Jews), the Nazis established a number of extermination camps in Poland, the country with the largest Jewish population. The extermination camps were designed for efficient mass murder. Chelmno, the first extermination camp, opened in December 1941. Jews and Roma were gassed in mobile gas vans there. In 1942, the Nazis opened the Belzec, Sobibor, and Treblinka extermination camps to systematically murder the Jews of the *Generalgouvernement* (the territory in the interior of occupied Poland).

Jews in Nazi occupied lands often were first deported to transit camps such as Westerbork in the Netherlands, or Drancy in France, en route to the killing centers in occupied Poland. The transit camps were usually the last stop before deportation to an extermination camp.

Millions of people were imprisoned and abused in the various types of Nazi camps. Under SS management, the Germans and their collaborators murdered more than three million Jews in the extermination camps alone. Only a small fraction of those imprisoned in Nazi camps survived.

When the Nazis invaded the Soviet Union in 1941, mobile killing units began to carry out mass-murders. The Nazis would also march thousands of Jews in to ravines and shoot them. These outdoor massacres accounted for over 1.3 million deaths.

When the Final Solution was put in to play by the Nazis, the systematic murder of millions of Jews would begin (and end with the murder of six million Jews).

The Final Solution

The Final Solution was put in effect after a meeting with Senior Nazi officials in January of 1942. During this time the Nazi's decided to begin closing ghettos and send their residents to extermination camps.

Talk of the Final Solution began to surface among top Nazi leadership in the summer of 1941, and this is when Adolph Eichmann first heard the of the Nazis future plan. He would later be put in charge of the mass deportations of Jews to extermination camps and be a key figure in the Final Solution.

On January 20, 1942, Eichmann was one of fifteen Nazi leaders that attended the Wannsee Conference where the formal pact was drawn between the political leadership and the bureaucracy to send European Jewry to the deaths. They would have to be assembled for easy transport to make the massive amount of deaths done efficiently.

Eichmann's principal concern was to keep the capacity of the killing in camps in high gear by maintaining a steady flow of victims. First into the gas chambers were children, mothers, and the old.

Deportations of Jews from the ghettos began happening from west to east. Jews were packed in trains from Germany, Holland, and Belgium with all going to Poland. Some people jumped from the death trains and survived. People who stayed on the trains immediately ended up in the death camps.

The extermination camps in Poland were Belzec, Chelmno, Majdanek, Sobibor, Treblinka, and Auschwitz. The camps were chosen because they were close to rail lines, which was important for having the most victims get to them as fast as possible.

During this time entire ghettos were closed down, and the most horrible acts of genocide in human history were being committed.

As soon as the trains would arrive, men and women were separated. Everyone was stripped of their clothing and valuables and put in to two groups, broken down by those who were put immediately in to the gas chambers (which were disguised as showers), and those who were chosen for horrific medical experiments or slave labor.

After being killed in the gas chambers, bodies were then stripped of hair, gold fillings, and teeth, and burned in crematoriums or buried in mass graves. These were used for used for rugs, socks, and mattresses.

In the camps, the lucky that were not immediately gassed were put into windowless barracks with no insulation. The only bathroom available was a bucket that everyone had to share, and in some cases there were 55 people in a barrack. Prisoners became diseased and dehydrated, as the living conditions were terrible and food was scarce.

Besides extermination camps, there were also many concentration camps established for slave labor. Prisoners here were subject to unstable working conditions and starvation.

Many people who learned about the camps wondered why the prisoners did not revolt, since there were many more prisoners then guards. There were some uprisings, but many of the Jews did not know that they were going to be killed and thought that they were just going to be doing forced labor. There were also many languages being spoken because prisoners came from all across Europe, and many of them lacked any military or organizational structure. In many situations, if someone did try to escape, guards would kill their entire family, or kill multiple people for ones act. Nobody wanted to be responsible for guards killing any number of people on account of them.

Adolf Eichmann zealously and efficiently organized the arrest and deportations of millions of Jews to death and concentration camps. Convinced of the importance and necessity of his task, he asserted that he performed his job with all the fanaticism that an old Nazi would expect of himself. He found his work fascinating and admitted doing it well gave him uncommon joy.

By 1944, Eichmann had reported that some four million Jews were killed in the camps and some two million more had been shot or killed by mobile units.

Suffering and Liberation

In late 1944, the Allied Forces began taking many areas across Germany. As the Allied Forces began to spread closer to the areas of Germany where the concentration and extermination camps were located, the Nazis began to take the prisoners from the camps and put them on death marches. The Nazis wanted to make sure that no one survived and also wanted to get rid of evidence of what they had been doing to the prisoners. The Nazis would torch the camps as they left for the death marches.

The death marches passed through many towns, and many of the prisoners died in front of townspeople and occasionally would die literally on the townspeople's doorsteps. Many of the Jews were shot during the marches, while others died from starvation, exhaustion, and the cold.

The death marches were carried out during the last ten months of the war, and an estimated 250,000 concentration camp prisoners were murdered or died as a result. The survivors of these marches would continue to suffer more after their liberation and after the war.

In the late spring/early summer of 1945, Allied forces began arriving in concentration camps. Nobody could have imagined the horror of what they were going to witness. When the Allies arrived at the camps they would find hundreds of thousands of suits, clothing, and thousands of pounds of human hair. What survivors were left, were found in a skeletal state and near death. Many of the prisoners were unable to eat or digest the food they were given by their rescuers, and died shortly after.

After the Third Reich's collapse in May of 1945, many concentration camps were turned into displaced person camps.

Nazi war records and official government documents from all over Europe place the death toll of the Holocaust at anywhere from ten million to twenty-six million people. In Poland, ninety percent of the Jewish population was killed.

Many victims of the Holocaust have stated that the atrocities happened in full public view, and that a big part of the continuing problem was that people looked the other way. Although the full amount of horrific acts were not confirmed to people until after the war, there were many rumors and eyewitness accounts across the world (even the United States) about the murder of many Jews and what was really happening in the camps.

The damage the Nazis did to the Jewish population was devastating and unmatched. The Nazis came very close to wiping out the entire Jewish population of Europe. In Poland, Germany, Austria, and in Baltic countries, nine out of every ten Jews were murdered. Of the nine million estimated Jews across Europe, roughly six million were killed.

With the end of WWII and the collapse of the Nazi regime, survivors of the Holocaust were faced with the daunting task of rebuilding their lives. Although survivors knew that they would never be able to fully recover mentally from the hardships they had to endure, they had to pick up whatever pieces were left of their lives and rebuild. Without financial resources and few, if any, surviving family members, most survivors eventually emigrated from Europe to start their lives over with a new hope of freedom and safety.

The preferred country of choice for almost all the Jews that were displaced/survived the Holocaust was Israel. For many survivors, the dream of going to Israel would eventually come true.

The majority of survivors did not want to return to their pre-war homes not only because their countries were in shambles and they didn't trust the locals, but because it was unsafe for them to return home. There were Jews that had been murdered by mobs when they attempted to return to Poland. People in the local community now occupied many of the Jews old homes, and they were hostile towards the Jews taking back what was theirs. While attempting to go home they would be met with protest and violence.

Several hundred thousand Jews became "Displaced Persons" and spent their time in makeshift camps, some of which were located at former concentration camps. These Displaced Persons camps were established throughout Europe. Medical personnel were brought into the camps to care for the victims and food supplies were provided. Even with this support, conditions in the camps were dismal.

When available, nearby SS living quarters were used as hospitals. Victims had no method of contacting relatives, because they were not allowed to send or receive mail.

Word of the poor treatment of Holocaust survivors in Displaced Persons camps had eventually reached Washington. President Truman, anxious to appease concerns, sent Earl G. Harrison, the dean of the University of Pennsylvania Law School, to Europe to investigate the camps.

Harrison was shocked by the appalling conditions he found once he arrived. Following Harrison's report of the condition and needs of refugees, President Truman called for major changes to the treatment of Jews in the camps.

Jews who were Displaced Persons originally did not have separate status as Jews, but were grouped together with other people from their original countries raising even more safety concerns.

General Dwight D. Eisenhower complied with Truman's request and began to implement changes in the camps, making them more humanitarian. Jews became a separate group in the camps so Polish Jews no longer had to live with other Poles and German Jews no longer had to live with Germans. In some cases, the Germans in these camps were previously guards in the concentration camps, yet they were still thrown in groups with the Jews.

Overall, Displaced Persons overwhelmingly wanted to go to Israel (Palestine). In a survey taken by the Displaced Persons, many indicated their first choice of migration was to Israel and their second choice of destination was also Israel.

In one camp, victims where told to pick a different second location and not to write Israel a second time. A significant portion then wrote *crematoria*.

Trouble in eastern Europe in 1946 more than doubled the number of Displaced Persons. At the beginning of the war, about 150,000 Polish Jews escaped to the Soviet Union.

In 1946, these Jews began being repatriated to Poland. There were reasons enough for Jews not to want to remain in Poland but one incident in particular convinced them to emigrate. On July 4, 1946, there was a pogrom against the Jews of Kielce and forty-one people were killed and sixty were seriously injured. By the winter of 1946 and 1947, there were about a quarter of a million Displaced Persons in Europe, and they all wanted to go to Israel.

Making Aliyah with my family on the way to Israel

Aliyah

The Jews had been returning to Jerusalem and the Holy Land through multiple Aliyah's (return to Israel) for many years. Many of these were older and less known pre-zionist Aliyahs that had taken place for hundreds and thousands of years. From groups of Jews (50,000) returning to Jerusalem from Babylon in 538BCE, to communities returning during the persecutions of the crusades beginning in 1100AD. Many Aliyah's lasted from 1200-1882, before the beginning of the Zionist Aliyah's with the Biluim from Russia in 1882.

In 1799, Napoleon issued a proclamation for a Jewish state in Palestine as a national homeland under French protection. Although he was defeated and forced to withdraw French troops, the idea caught the attention of many, especially the British who would later declare a Jewish homeland.

Large modern exposure to Zionism, (a policy for establishing and developing a national Jewish homeland took form in February of 1896 when *Der Judenstaat* (The Jewish State), by Theodore Herzl was published in Germany. By May, the English version was released. The book outlined Herzl's answer to the "Jewish Question", which was to establish a Jewish state.

"The Jewish State" is considered one of the most important texts of early Zionism. Herzl envisioned the founding of a future independent Jewish state during the 20th century. He argued that the best way to avoid anti-semitism in Europe was to create this independent Jewish state.

Herzl made the term Zionism popular and become a recognized leader of the Zionist movement, which grew drastically. Herzl headed the first Zionist congress in 1897, which took place in Basel, Switzerland and featured hundreds of delegates representing 17 different countries. The delegates were from multiple different Zionist societies. They adopted the Hatikvah as their anthem, and it would later become the anthem of the State of Israel many years later.

In 1897, after the event in Basel, Hershel wrote in his diary:

"Were I to sum up the Basle Congress in a word - which I shall guard against pronouncing publicly - it would be this: At Basle I founded the Jewish State. If I said this out loud today I would be greeted by universal laughter. In five years perhaps, and certainly in fifty years, everyone will perceive it."

Turkey's Ottoman empire had owned Lebanon, Syria, and Palestine from 1517-1917. During WW1, the Ottoman Empire supported Germany, so when Germany lost, the Ottoman Empire also lost.

In 1916. control of the southern portion of the Ottoman Empire was mandated to France and Britain through the Sykes-Picot Agreement, which divided the Arab region into zones of influence. Lebanon and Syria were mandated to France, while "Palestine" or today's Jordan, Israel, and the West Bank were mandated to Great Britain.

Nobody had established a homeland in the area since the Jews had done it 2,000 years before, so the British looked favorably on the creation of a Jewish National Homeland throughout all of the land.

The Jews had already begun mass immigration in the late 1800s in an effort to rid the land of swamps and malaria and prepare for the rebirth of Israel. This Jewish effort to revitalize the land attracted an equally large immigration of Arabs from neighboring areas that were drawn by employment opportunities and healthier living conditions.

There was never any attempt to rid the area of what few Arabs there were, or the Arab masses that immigrated into the area with the Jews.

In 1917, the British government made a formal statement of policy in establishing a National Jewish homeland. It was made in a letter by the Foreign Secretary Arthur James Balfour, and was made out to *Lord Rothschild*, who was Walter Rothschild (the 2nd Baron Rothschild).

Rothschild was a leader in the Jewish community and was given the letter to pass on to the *Zionist Federation of Great Britain and*

Ireland. This was an umbrella organization that encompassed most of the Zionist organizations, which was the representation of the Zionist organizations in the United Kingdom.

The Balfour Declaration:

Foreign Office,
November 2nd, 1917.

Dear Lord Rothschild,

I have much pleasure in conveying to you, on behalf of His Majesty's Government, the following declaration of sympathy with Jewish Zionist aspirations which has been submitted to, and approved by, the Cabinet:
"His Majesty's Government view with favour the establishment in Palestine of a national home for the Jewish people, and will use their best endeavours to facilitate the achievement of this object, it being clearly understood that nothing shall be done which may prejudice the civil and religious rights of existing non-Jewish communities in Palestine, or the rights and political status enjoyed by Jews in any other country".
I should be grateful if you would bring this declaration to the knowledge of the Zionist Federation.

Yours sincerely,
Arthur James Balfour

While many Jews were continuing to make Aliyah, especially after the time of the Balfour Declaration, Arabs began to not like the idea of Palestine being a Jewish homeland.

In 1922, Winston Churchill created what would be known as the Churchill White Papers of 1922. These papers were released to describe more in depth what the Balfour Declaration stated. It was a document that further explained the quote of the "Establishment in Palestine of a national home for the Jewish people".

The papers explained that it was not Britain's idea to make the area "as Jewish as England in English". The papers outlined making a National Home for the Jewish people, but while stating that they were to live alongside the Arabs in unity.

These papers were to outline that the British Government did not support the Jewish people having full power, but wanted to allow them to be able to freely immigrate to make it their national homeland but not their own State.

There had been a steady flow of rioting by the Arabs, and a report (The Shaw Report) was commissioned to find out what the Arabs were angry about to get to the source of the problem. The report found that the Arab's complaints and blames on the Jews were ridiculous and untrue. One complaint was that the Jews were buying all of the Arab's fertile land, when in fact, much of the land then carrying orange groves were initially sand dunes or swamp and was uncultivated when it was purchased. It was found that the previous Arab owners did not have the resources or training needed to develop the land. Another complaint was that the giant amount of Jewish immigrants were making it hard for the Palestinians to have their land, when in fact it was not the Jews, but the large number of Arabs immigrating to the country that were creating the problem.

In reaction to mass Jewish immigration was the Arab Revolt, which lasted from 1936-1939. The Arabs were mad about the British rule, and about the ever-growing number of Jews.

As Jews continued to immigrate, new White Papers were released in 1939, whereas Britain decided that since 450,000 Jews had immigrated, the Balfour Agreement's terms had been met.
From the new White Papers, Britain outlined that there would be an independent state within ten years, governed by both the Arabs and the Jews. The British wanted to have both communities be able to rule together as a safeguard for each of their interests.

The White Papers of 1939 also put restrictions on the sale of land from Arabs to Jews. The Jewish population was buying enormous amounts of land from Arabs and the British believed it was getting to a point where if there were not restrictions, there would not be any more land for the Arab population to own.

The final major restriction that the White Papers had was that of immigration of Jews. The Jews were to not have more then 75,000 immigrants for the next five years, after which time their immigration numbers would depend on Arab consent. The 75,000 allowed were explained as no more then 10,000 people a year for five years, then if the High Commander was satisfied with there being adequate room for immigrants, 25,000 could enter afterwards.

The immigration cap began happening while Nazis were persecuting Jews across Europe, making the timing an even bigger problem. In attempt to save Jewish lives in Europe, Zionist organizations began to setup Illegal Immigration operations.

Britain's refusal to allow Displaced Persons into the area was plagued with problems. Illegal immigration was called Aliyah Bet, meaning Aliyah "B" because the name given to legal immigration to Israel was Aliyah Aleph, or Aliyah "A". In modern day Israel, Aliyah Bet is known as *Ha'apala*. Many Jews that took part in this form of immigration refuse to call it illegal, but instead *clandestine*.

There were two different phases of Ha'apala. The first phase was from 1934 to 1942, and the main objective during this period was to help European Jews escape the Nazis. After the war, until 1948, the main objective was to find homes for the Jewish survivors of the Nazi's who were scattered among the millions of Displaced Persons in Germany.

During the first phase, there were many different organizations that took part in attempting to save the Jews from the Nazi's. After the war, the *Mossad LeAliyah Bet* (The Institute for Aliyah B) specifically took over the operations of saving the Jewish survivors and finding them homes in Israel.

Jews formed an organization called *Bricha* (flight) for the purpose of smuggling immigrants. Jews were moved to Italy. From Italy, ships and crews were rented for the passage across the Mediterranean. Some of the ships made it past a British naval blockade of the area, but most did not. The passengers of captured ships were forced to disembark in Cyprus, where the British operated Displaced Person camps.

After Jews were shipped to Cyprus were then able to apply for legal immigration. The British Royal Army ran the camps on the island. Armed patrols guarded the perimeters to prevent escape. 52,000 Jews were interned and 2200 babies were born on Cyprus between 1946 and 1949 on the island. Approximately eighty percent of the internees were between the ages of thirteen and thirty-five. Jewish organization was strong in Cyprus and education and job training became provided internally. Leaders on Cyprus often became initial government officials in the eventual new state of Israel.

Formation of Israel

Overwhelmed by international pressures and opinions, Britain placed the matter of the Jewish homeland into the hands of the United Nations in February 1947. In the fall of 1947, the General Assembly voted to partition the area and create two independent states, one Jewish and the other Arab. Fighting immediately broke out between Jews and Arabs. Even with the United Nations decision, Britain still kept firm control of Palestinian immigration.

On May 14th, 1948, the British government left, and the State of Israel was proclaimed the same day. The United States was the first country to recognize the new State. Legal immigration began in earnest, even though the Israeli parliament, the Knesset, did not approve the "Law of Return," which allows any Jew to migrate to Israel and become a citizen, until July 1950.

On May 15th, 1948, the day after the creation of the State of Israel, Egypt, Iraq, Jordan, Lebanon, Saudi Arabia, and Syria attacked Israel from all sides. Although the Arab armies were larger and better equipped then Israel's, Israel gained control of the war against the Arab countries. Fighting officially ended in January of 1949. Between January and July of 1949, agreements were created between Israel and Egypt, Lebanon, Syria, and Jordan. Israel had hoped that their armistice agreements would lead to official Arab-Israeli peace treaties, but the Arab States had decided to not recognize Israel's existence. After the 'War of Independence', Israel had the original 5,600 square miles of land that the UN had originally partitioned to them, alongside an extra 2,500 square miles.

Despite war against Arab neighbors, immigration to Israel increased rapidly. On May 15, 1948, the first day of Israeli statehood, 1,700 immigrants arrived. There was an average of 13,500 immigrants each month from May through December of 1948, far exceeding the prior legal migration approved by the British of 1,500 per month. Ultimately, the survivors of the Holocaust were able to immigrate to Israel. The State of Israel accepted as many Jews that were willing to come.

Between 1948 and 1951, nearly 700,000 Jews immigrated to the new state of Israel. Approximately 140,000 Holocaust survivors came to America after 1948, most settling in New York.

Although Israel had been established, there would continue to be multiple Arab attacks on the new Jewish State.

Foreign Office,
November 2nd, 1917.

Dear Lord Rothschild,

I have much pleasure in conveying to you, on behalf of His Majesty's Government, the following declaration of sympathy with Jewish Zionist aspirations which has been submitted to, and approved by, the Cabinet

"His Majesty's Government view with favour the establishment in Palestine of a national home for the Jewish people, and will use their best endeavours to facilitate the achievement of this object, it being clearly understood that nothing shall be done which may prejudice the civil and religious rights of existing non-Jewish communities in Palestine, or the rights and political status enjoyed by Jews in any other country"

I should be grateful if you would bring this declaration to the knowledge of the Zionist Federation.

Suez War

In the fall of 1948, the United Nations Security Council called on Israel and the Arab states to negotiate agreements to stop their fighting. Egypt agreed, but only after Israel had routed its army and driven to El Arish in the Sinai. At the time, the British were ready to defend Egypt under an Anglo-Egyptian treaty. Rather than accept the humiliation of British assistance, however, the Egyptians met the Israelis at Rhodes, a Greek island southwest of Turkey, for negotiations.

By the summer of 1949, armistice agreements had been negotiated between Israel, Egypt, Jordan, Lebanon and Syria. Iraq, who had also fought against Israel, refused to follow suit. The success at Rhodes was due to it being insisted that there would be direct bilateral talks between Israel and each Arab state.

On September 1, 1951, the Security Council ordered Egypt to open the Canal to Israeli shipping. Egypt refused to comply. The Egyptian Foreign Minister, Muhammad Salah al-Din, said early in 1954:

"The Arab people will not be embarrassed to declare: We shall not be satisfied except by the final obliteration of Israel from the map of the Middle East."

In 1955, Egyptian President Gamal Abdel Nassar began to import arms from the Soviet Bloc to build his arsenal for the confrontation with Israel. In the short-term, however, he employed a new tactic to prosecute Egypt's war with Israel. He announced it on August 31, 1955:

"Egypt has decided to dispatch her heroes, the disciples of Pharaoh and the sons of Islam and they will cleanse the land of Palestine....there will be no peace on Israel's border because we demand vengeance, and vengeance is Israel's death."

These so-called heroes were Arab terrorists, or *Fedayeen*, trained and equipped by Egyptian Intelligence to engage in hostile action on the border and infiltrate Israel to commit acts of sabotage and murder. The Fedayeen operated mainly from bases in Jordan, so that Jordan would bear the brunt of Israel's retaliation, which inevitably followed. The terrorist attacks violated the armistice agreement provision that prohibited the initiation of hostilities by paramilitary forces; nevertheless, it was Israel that was condemned by the United Nations Security Council for its counter attacks.

In 1956, three of the twentieth century's most dominant forces came together in a short, violent clash in the Egyptian regions known as the Suez Canal and the Sinai Peninsula. These three forces or themes were nationalism, the Cold War and the Arab-Israeli conflict.

Egypt and other Arab nations had recently gained full independence from the empires controlled by European powers such as Great Britain and France. These young nations with ancient cultures and histories strove to gain economic and military sufficiency while asserting their political rights as free peoples.

The Cold War struggle between the mostly democratic and capitalist West against the Communist East dominated by the Soviet Union and China both helped and hindered the Nationalist goals of many African and Asian countries. An example is that Egypt sought foreign aid in building the Aswan Dam project, which would control the wild Nile River. The United States and Britain, who were the major players in the West, declined to help Egypt because of her political and military ties to the Soviet Union. The Soviets eagerly rushed in to aid Egypt. After this, Egypt came to be considered a friend of the Soviets, and a nation not overly friendly to the West. In this way, the Cold War affected the young nation of Egypt and her relations with the rest of the world. The Arab-Israeli conflict began in 1948 and caused Egypt and Israel to be bitter enemies until 1979. The second war between these Middle East neighbors took place in 1956.

As part of Egyptian President Nasser's nationalist agenda, he took control of the Suez Canal zone away from the British and French companies which owned it. At the same time, as part of his ongoing struggle with Israel, Egyptian forces blocked the Straits of Tiran, the narrow waterway that was Israel's only outlet to the Red Sea.

Israel and Egypt had clashed repeatedly since their 1948 war as Egypt allowed and encouraged groups of Palestinian fighters to attack Israel from Egyptian territory. In response, Israeli forces constantly made cross-border raids in retaliation. Britain and France, both of whom were in the process of losing their centuries-old empires, decided on a strategy straight out of their 19th Century Imperial histories. Their plan led to a joint invasion and occupation of the Suez Canal zone by Britain and France. This was meant to reassert control of this vital waterway to the British and French companies stung by Nasser's bold nationalization. At France's suggestion, planning was coordinated with Israel, a fact, which all three nations denied for years afterwards.

On October 29, 1956, Israeli troops invaded Egypt's Sinai Peninsula and quickly overcame opposition as they raced for Suez. The next day, Britain and France, following their part of the script, offered to temporarily occupy the Canal Zone and suggested a ten mile buffer on either side, which would separate the Egyptian forces from the Israelis.

Nasser refused the buffer, and on October 31, Egypt was attacked and invaded by the military forces of Britain and France. In response to these developments, the Soviet Union, which at the time was ruthlessly suppressing an anti-Communist uprising in Hungary, threatened to intervene on Egypt's behalf. President Eisenhower of the United States pressured Britain, France, and Israel into agreeing to a cease-fire and eventual withdrawal from Egypt.

The United States, caught by surprise by the dual invasions, was more concerned with the Soviet war in Hungary and the Cold War than with Britain and France's dealings involving Suez. The last thing President Eisenhower wanted was a wider war over Suez. The war itself lasted for only a week, and invading forces were withdrawn within the month. As a result, Egypt now firmly aligned herself with the Soviet Union, which armed Egypt and other Arab nations for the continuing struggle against Israel.

Through the new Israeli governments constant problems with the Arabs (especially Egypt), the citizens and children of Israel were on the defense on a regular basis. Many of the children of Israel had not known in depth about what their parents had went through a few years earlier during the Holocaust because of the silence they had used to go forward without the setbacks from their painful memories.

As the wars in the middle east were ensuing, there were parts of the Israeli military and intelligence that made it a goal to hunt down the war criminal Nazis that had escaped Europe after WWII. If the ongoing wars were not enough pressure on the children of Israel, soon their parent's past would be revealed through the war trials.

Eichmann Trial

The Trials

After WWII, many war criminals fled to countries that were willing to offer amnesty and would not extredite them even though they were fully aware of the atrocities that these individuals committed. Most of the big war criminals went into hiding in Argentina and Western Europe.

Throughout the 1950s, many Jews and other victims of the Holocaust dedicated themselves to finding Eichmann and other notorious Nazis. Among them was the Jewish Nazi hunter Simon Wiesenthal. In 1954, Wiesenthal received a postcard from an associate living in Buenos Aires informing him that Eichmann was in Argentina.

The message read in part:

> *Ich sah jenes schmutzige Schwein Eichmann. ("I saw that filthy pig Eichmann.") Er wohnt in der Nähe von Buenos Aires und*

*arbeitet für ein Wassergeschäft. ("He lives near Buenos Aires
and works for a water company.")*

Adolf Eichmann changed his name but strangely never changed
those of his wife and four children. It was this mistake that led to
his eventual capture by the Israeli secret services. In 1959, the
Mossad was informed that Eichmann was in Buenos Aires under
the alias Ricardo Klement and began an immediete effort to locate
his exact whereabouts. Through relentless surveillance, it was
concluded that Ricardo Klement was, in fact, Adolf Eichmann.

The Israeli government then approved an operation to capture
Eichmann and bring him to Jerusalem for trial as a war criminal.
The Mossad agents continued their surveillance of Eichmann
through the first months of 1960 until it was judged safe to take
him down. Eichmann was captured by a team of Mossad and Shin
Bet agents in a suburb of Buenos Aires on May 11, 1960, as part
of a covert operation. The Mossad agents had arrived in Buenos
Aires in April 1960 after Eichmann's identity was confirmed.

Eichmann's trial before an Israeli court in Jerusalem began on
April 11, 1961. He was indicted on 15 criminal charges, including

crimes against humanity, crimes against the Jewish people, and membership in an outlawed organization.

In accordance with Israeli criminal procedure, the trial was presided over by three judges: Moshe Landau, Benjamin Halevi, and Yitzhak Raveh. The chief prosecutor was Gideon Hausner, the Israeli attorney general. The three judges sat high atop a plain dais. The trial was held at the *Beit Ha'am*—today known as the Gerard Behar Center—a new auditorium in downtown Jerusalem. Eichmann sat inside a bulletproof glass booth to protect him from victims' families. The legal basis of the charges against Eichmann was the 1950 *Nazi and Nazi Collaborators (Punishment) Law*.

The trial caused huge international controversy, as well as an international sensation. The Israeli government allowed news programs all over the world to broadcast the trial live with few restrictions. The trial began with various witnesses, including many Holocaust survivors, who testified against Eichmann and his role in transporting victims to the extermination camps. One key witness for the prosecution was an American judge named Michael A. Musmanno, who was a U.S. naval officer in 1945. Musmanno had questioned the Nuremberg defendants and would later go on to become a Justice of the Pennsylvania Supreme

Court. He testified that the late Hermann Göring "made it very clear that Eichmann was the man to determine, in what order, in what countries, the Jews were to die."

When the prosecution rested, Eichmann's defense lawyers, Robert Servatius and Dieter Wechtenbruch, opened up the defense by explaining why they did not cross-examine any of the prosecution witnesses. Eichmann, speaking in his own defense, said that he did not dispute the facts of what happened during the Holocaust. During the whole trial, Eichmann insisted that he was only "following orders from his superiors"—the same defense used by some of the Nazi war criminals during the 1945–1946 Nuremberg Trials.

He explicitly declared that he had abdicated his conscience in order to follow the *Führerprinzip* (meaning that Hitlers word was above all written law). Eichmann claimed that he was merely a "transmitter" with very little power. He testified that: "I never did anything, great or small, without obtaining in advance express instructions from Adolf Hitler or any of my superiors."

During cross-examination, prosecutor Hausner asked Eichmann if he considered himself guilty of the murder of millions of Jews. Eichmann replied: "Legally not, but in the human sense ... yes, for I am guilty of having deported them." When Hausner produced as evidence a quote by Eichmann in 1945 stating: "I will leap into my grave laughing because the feeling that I have five million human beings on my conscience is for me a source of extraordinary satisfaction." Eichmann countered the claim saying that he was referring only to "enemies of the Reich".

Witnesses for the defense, all of them former high-ranking Nazis, were promised immunity and safe conduct from their German and Austrian homes to testify in Jerusalem on Eichmann's behalf. All of them refused to travel to Israel, but they sent the court depositions. None of the depositions supported Eichmann's following orders defense.

One deposition was from Otto Winkelmann, a former senior SS police leader in Budapest in 1944. His memo stated that "[Eichmann] had the nature of a subaltern, which means a fellow who uses his power recklessly, without moral restraints. He would certainly overstep his authority if he thought he was acting in the spirit of his commander [Adolf Hitler]".

Franz Six, a former SS brigadier general in the German secret service -who was assigned the supervision of the occupation of the United Kingdom had Operation Sea Lion been successful- said in his deposition that Eichmann was an absolute believer in National Socialism and would act to the most extreme of the party doctrine. He also stated that Eichmann had greater power than other department chiefs.

After fourteen weeks of testimony with more than 1,500 documents, 100 prosecution witnesses (ninety of whom were Nazi concentration camp survivors), and dozens of defense depositions delivered by diplomatic couriers from sixteen different countries, the Eichmann trial ended on August 14. At that point, the judges began deliberations in seclusion. On December 11, the three judges announced their verdict: Eichmann was found guilty and convicted on all counts. Eichmann had said to the court that he expected to be convited and sentenced to death.

On December 15, the court imposed a death sentence. Eichmann appealed the verdict, mostly relying on legal arguments about Israel's jurisdiction and the legality of the laws under which he was charged. He also claimed that he was protected by the principle of "Acts of State" and repeated his "following orders" defense.

On May 29, 1962 Israel's Supreme Court, sitting as a Court of Criminal Appeal, rejected the appeal and upheld the District Court's judgment on all counts. In rejecting his appeal again claiming that he was only "following orders", the court stated that, "Eichmann received no superior orders at all. He was his own superior and he gave all orders in matters that concerned Jewish affairs ... the so-called Final Solution would never have assumed the infernal forms of the flayed skin and tortured flesh of millions of Jews without the fanatical zeal and the unquenchable blood thirst of the appellant and his associates." A large number of prominent persons sent requests for clemency.

On May 31, Israeli President Yitzhak Ben-Zvi turned down Eichmann's petition for mercy. On the telegram that Eichmann's wife, Vera, sent in support of the clemency, Ben-Zvi added in his handwriting a passage from the First Book of Samuel: "As your sword bereaved women, so will your mother be bereaved among women." (1 Samuel 15:33, Samuel's words to Agag, king of the Amalekites).

Eichmann was hung minutes before midnight on May 31, 1962, at a prison in Ramla, Israel. This remains the only civil execution ever carried out in Israel, which has a general policy of not using the death penalty. Eichmann allegedly refused a last meal, preferring instead a bottle of Carmel, a dry red Israeli wine. He consumed about half of the bottle. He also refused to don the traditional black hood for his execution.

Shortly after the execution, Eichmann's body was cremated in a specially designed furnace. The furnace was so hot that no one dared to go near it. A stretcher on tracks was used to put the body in.

The next morning, on June 1, his ashes were scattered at sea over the Mediterranean, beyond the territorial waters of Israel by an Israeli Navy patrol boat. This was to ensure that there could be no future memorial and that no country would serve as his final resting place.

Psychological Effects on Survivors

The Holocaust was one of the most tragic events in the history of mankind. The affects did not just appear on the fortunate survivors, but everyone around them.

The survivors might be considered very lucky to have made it through all the atrocities from Nazi Germany, but there are times when their memories and flashbacks have made them wish they were the ones who died instead of living with the horrible aftermath of the war and its affect on their hearts, minds, and souls.

The psychological effects of the Holocaust on survivors from different aspects and parts of the war (such as survivors of ghettos and camps) are different in some ways, but in others, extremely similar. The gigantic number of prisoners with backgrounds of many different nationalities and religions in the camps helped to make these differences inevitable.

The long-range psychological effects of the Holocaust on the mental health of survivors are very immense and complex. There is no doubt that many people suffered from a very profound shock that was put through everyone arriving at the death camps.

At the death camps, many people who had heard rumors were now staring them right in the eye and seeing that they were very true. Shock was followed by apathy. A famous psychoanalyst Martin Wangh has said, "recovery from these two states could occur only by a means of psychic splitting. This meant that some form of denial or 'psychic numbing,' 'derealization,' or 'depersonalization' had to take place."

The senses of the prisoners grew, and mentally they had to live like a hunted animal because they were always on the alert for danger.

Any feeling of aggression or vengeance had to be hidden, and from this a paranoid attitude could develop deep within each prisoner.

Hiding emotions and being unable to grasp what was going on around them was a period filled with extreme danger. New arrivals from the camps were already exhausted from the dehumanizing conditions from their transport or living in ghettos, and if they stayed in this shock for a long length of time, they would be looked at as weak, and most likely killed.

Due to the traumatization of the Holocaust, in order for the victims to resist dehumanization and regression and to find support, they had to share stories about the past, fantasies about the future and joint prayers as well as poetry and expressions of personal and general human aspirations for hope and love. Imagination was an important means of liberation from the frustrating reality by creating an outlet of positive plans for the distant future in their minds, and by spurring to immediate actions.

One way survivors coped with the constant horrors of the Holocaust was to keep up hope in reuniting with their families.

After liberation, most of them were confronted not only with the discovery that their family members and friends had all been killed, but also learned the horrible circumstances of their deaths. Many survivors, when physically able, returned to their hometowns only to find their property destroyed or taken over, their pre-war neighbors hostile, and their communities obliterated.

Some continued their search in the Displaced Persons camps and elsewhere in Europe for several years. While some did find a few surviving relatives, others either never discovered what happened to their loved ones or learned that every single Jewish person they had ever known before the war had been murdered. Many survivors were unable to fully comprehend their tragedy or to express their grief or rage, but still had to undertake the task of rebuilding their lives.

As they began their new lives, living conditions were often cramped and poor. There were few clothes and household goods available and food was rationed. Interesting and well-paying jobs were hard to come by. Most of the young refugees found themselves in factory or office jobs, or in domestic work.

A frequent occurrence was marriages that were "created" very fast, instead of people taking awhile to get to know their future spouse. Recreating a family and bringing a child into the world was a strong attempt to compensate for their losses and to undo the dehumanization and loneliness they had experienced. Many survivors gave birth in Displaced Persons camps as soon as they were physically able to. Newborn children were named after the family members who had died. The children were often viewed as a symbol of victory over the Nazis because they were the future.

Uprooted, dislocated, and robbed, most survivors decided to leave Europe and find a safer place to live and rebuild their lives. Many Jews survived the war with a strong belief in Zionism and went to Israel. Others, who had relatives in North America, went there with the hope of recreating an extended family.

In the United States, the majority of survivors encountered a negative reaction and attitude from people. Most arrived as penniless refugees and received initial financial aid from relatives and Jewish organizations. The survivors were provided with very little help in emotional rehabilitation because their war stories were too horrifying for most people to listen to.

Many bystander's guilt for having knowingly neglected to do anything to help the Holocaust survivors made many people believe that survivors were pointing a finger at them. Reactions such as "that's in the past", "let bygones be bygones", "be grateful and happy for getting to America", or "look at the positive side of things" caused most survivors to keep silent.

The beginning of the silence was important to the psychological well being of the survivors, their families, and to them integrating into new cultures. At the same time, silence increased survivors' senses of isolation, and extended their own mourning processes. The only option left to survivors, other than sharing their Holocaust experiences with each other, was to withdraw completely into their newly established families. It has only been within the last 10 to 15 years that people have wanted to hear, but now many of the adult survivors have already passed away.

A syndrome is a group of signs or symptoms that occur together and characterize an abnormality. After World War II, the medical profession in many countries started to be confronted with survivors of the Nazi concentration camps. It took several years before a large scientifically based view of their problems could develop.

In 1961, William G. Nielderland, a famous psychoanalyst in the field of treating survivors, coined the term "Survivor Syndrome". He came to realize that the symptoms affected not only survivors, but their families as well. The normal symptoms included an inability to work, and even at times to talk. Anxieties and fears of renewed persecution, such as fearing uniformed police officers, were common. There were also many feelings of guilt for having survived when others had not. Survivors would wonder why they were able to be alive when their family members were not. The survivors had many symptoms involving thoughts of death, nightmares, panic attacks, and various other psychosomatic symptoms. Marital problems would combine with disinterest in life, people, and reality.

After many studies, five psychological themes in survivors were found. The first is the "death imprint", which is related to anxiety about death. It is not just a basic death, but grotesque and horrifying forms of death. For many survivors, the imagery can include many forms of memory -the smoke or smell of the gas chambers, the brutal killing of someone in a camp they witnessed, or the separation from a family member never seen again. The survivor can feel stuck in time and be unable to move beyond the pain in their mind.

The second category is "death guilt". Death guilt is taken from the question "why did I survive, while he, she, or they did not?" Before this happens, however, the imagery from the first theme of "death imprint" has already taken shape.

Part of the survivors' sense of horror is the memory of their own helplessness and inability to act in a way of saving people or resisting the Nazis, or be able to feel rage or compassion because they were so mentally numb. Death guilt begins in the gap between the physical and the psychological. Within the psychological imagery is the survivor's sense of debt to the dead and responsibility to them. Sometimes the survivors feel guiltier than the perpetrators. The sense of guilt can be especially strong concerning the death of close relatives or friends.

The third category of the survivor syndrome is "psychic numbing", which is the inability to feel. Psychologists have come to recognize psychic numbing as a necessary psychological defense against overwhelming images. However, this can easily outlive its usefulness and develop into withdrawal, apathy, depression, and despair. Many survivors describe having survived by losing all feeling.

The fourth category has to do with survivor sensitivity to or suspicion of "fake" people trying to help them. The survivor feels the effects of his or her ordeal, but frequently resents help that is offered because it is perceived as a sign of weakness. Following the death immersion experience, the survivor's sense of a fake universe may continue where they do not trust anyone. This sense seems to be confirmed when they realize that others view them as in some way carrying the taint of the Holocaust, as someone to be feared and avoided as though they were contagious. They may in some cases inwardly accept this social response and actually feel tainted themselves. These conflicts can lead to patterns of distrust in human relationships, and that the sense of the world around them or even life itself, is fake.

The fifth and final category is the survivor's "struggle for meaning". Survivors of Nazi death camps have been called collectors of justice because they are looking for something beyond economic or social restitution.

These survivors seek the acknowledgement of crimes committed against them and punishment of those responsible in order to reestablish at least the resemblance of a moral world. The impulse to bear witness, beginning with a sense of responsibility to the dead, can become a mission. For many survivors, the mission took the form of involvement in the creation of the State of Israel and their Zionist beliefs.

The Second Generation

A whole complex series of emotions surround the birth of each second-generation child. Many survivors were scared that they might not be able to have children because of what they experienced. Not being able to have a child was considered the ultimate defeat.

Once born, the second-generation children were bound to be special. A child was tangible evidence of not only one's own survival, but also the Jewish people, and therefore, incredibly precious. For many parents, the child represented the ultimate defeat of the Nazis; a life had been created against incredible odds. For others, the birth was a profoundly religious event and was a gift of God.

In the postwar world, the parents held high hopes for their children. Yet as magnificent as they were, the parents held both positive and negative feelings towards these children. The world had proven to be a dangerous place for them, especially because they were Jewish. One and a half million Jewish children had died in the Holocaust. For the survivors, an intense personal war continued in which the ultimate victory would be obtained through the success and survival of their children.

It was always traditional within Jewish families to invest everything into their children. Children have always been highly valued by Jewish parents. The mother, in particular, has always had a very important role in the upbringing of her children. Beginning at birth, the mother implanted foundational values of their heritage and of their own self-worth. But what about the mother and father who suffers from Survivors Syndrome? Because of their own difficulties, there was often severe impairment in their ability to respond appropriately to their growing child, set limits, encourage curiosity, and accept normal activity in their children.

The experiences of the parents in the Holocaust resulted in their viewing the child as a reversal of their own encounter with death and destruction. Consequently, the child was often "over valued and invested with meanings that were different from his own resources and abilities. He had placed on him expectations which far exceeded his own."

The second-generation child's accommodation of the parent's wishes was a critical ingredient to the parent's own psychological survival.

Parent's responses to their children varied. Some parents were unable to invest emotionally in their children. Many of these parents were too busy with mourning in their own losses. Many were emotionally spent and physically unable to be emotional with their children. Resources they may have been able to use in a bad situation previously through extended family were not available to these parents.

Other parents expected their children to be representatives or reincarnations of those who were lost. The survivor's children were not treated as individuals as much as a procession to provide meaning to the parent's emptied lives. The child was expected to vindicate all the suffering they had endured.

Many of the survivors had been married before the war and some even had children. As it is traditional in Judaism to name children after deceased relatives, new children were often named after deceased children from the pre-war family.

Such children live not only their own existence, but also the existence of their deceased brother, sister, parent, or grandparent. Second-generation children felt as if they were filling some one else's shoes or living with a ghost. Because of this, they were disciplined harshly growing up to achieve the parent's idealized version of the deceased relatives. Children who actually did very well for themselves were given no restrictions. The other siblings were then compared to that success and made to feel inadequate compared to them.

The parents' needs had been repressed or denied to such a great extent during the war that after the war their neediness overflowed. The parents' needs consequently became more important than the needs of their children. Many times it was as if the psychological needs of the parents depended on the conformity of the children. The need to restore lost relatives, coupled with the fear of experiencing another loss caused many parents to over invest in their children.

The children of survivors had known of their parents survivor-hood for as long as they could remember. Many children could not remember a time when they did not have at least a dim awareness of their parents' experiences of persecution. Most children, however, only had a small knowledge of some details. Some parents had withheld all information about their experiences in the past, while others constantly repeated stories about their past from the time their children were little. Even the parents that did talk about their experiences did not communicate a fully detailed picture about their lives before and during the Holocaust.

The responses of children to their parents' Holocaust accounts included "isolation, denial, horror, guilt, anger at the world, and anger at the parents for subjecting them to the horrors of the past". Most children were extremely hesitant to question their parents directly because they did not want to do their parents harm. Some children reported that knowledge of the parents suffering was very painful for them and produced in them a need to distance themselves. At the same time, many children were in awe of their parent's ability to endure in the face of the seemingly overwhelming conditions of the concentration camps.

Many of the themes that emerged from the parent/child relationship were the unavailability of the parents for their children's emotional needs, the extremely controlling and overprotective behavior of parents, and the induction of guilt feelings in the children. Parents communicated the idea that the only thing of value left in their lives was their children. The positive aspects of the parent/child relationships were that no child doubted his parent's love and all children saw their parents as consciously having their best interests in mind.

When the survivor's children were exposed to the Holocaust, they were also exposed to the stress of having to confront a cataclysm themselves. For these children, whose parents were still living with the scars of the Holocaust, the knowledge of the past was considered to be traumatic. The constant and stressful presence of concentration camp imagery and evidence of their parents suffering created a daily exposure. They would have to regularly see their parents' state of having been traumatized, and since they were so psychologically close to their parents it was like having been in a concentration camp themselves.

Bodies of prisoners killed

Physical Affects

The conditions of the camps were so terrible that it is hard to find words to describe them. Any attempt to describe them would be a gross understatement. The nutrition was so terrible that the survivors looked like living corpses, just skeletons covered with skin. It became virtually impossible to tell the prisoners apart.

If deaths from the gas chamber and crematoriums are not included, mortality was still extremely high from multiple infections, frost bite, injuries, disease of the respiratory tract, diarrhea, and first and foremost - chronic malnutrition and the diseases associated with it. Clothing and housing were worse than a third world countries prison. Lice and scabies infections were rampant, along with many other infectious diseases such as typhus.

After liberation, the diseases that were apparent were treated as best as could be done. However, some survivor's diseases and defective conditions had slowly developed in to new conditions that nobody could expect. They were not always potent, and the survivors never dramatized them to let the doctors know about their underlying condition. The connection between their sufferings in the camps and later illnesses was not obvious and doctors knew little about it. Physicians had never had the opportunity to see and examine corpses. The experiences in the camps were beyond any reach of imagination, and the results of their experiences were also completely unknown and unexpected.

The symptoms most frequently described were fatigue, memory loss, an inability to concentrate, restlessness, irritability, emotional liability, disturbance of sleep, headaches, and various vegetative symptoms. Anxiety and mood disorders were other aspects of the syndrome found in many of the investigated survivors. Slowly a general agreement as to the existence and disabling effects of this syndrome evolved.

One very common characteristic that doctors began to notice was that there was premature aging in survivors. The general impression in practically all the physicians dealing with these patients was that they looked older than their age.

Somatic disorders affecting several body systems were often apparent in the same patient. From this, there were two types of patients, those with diseases of the digestive tract, and those with cardiovascular diseases.

Diseases of the digestive tract were the most common, involving more than a third of the patients, with tendencies toward diarrhea and peptic ulcers being the most frequent. Peptic ulcers were most common in those who had shown signs of emotional disturbance after the war.

Cardiovascular diseases were the second most common. Most researchers believe that these diseases are more common, particularly coronary disease, cerebrovascular diseases, and other manifestations of arteriosclerosis. This would be consistent with the frequent findings of premature aging and the atrophy of the heart muscle due to undernourishment during captivity.

Diseases of the respiratory tract have only been recorded in thirty percent of the survivors. The general impression was that these former prisoners had developed a reduced resistance toward respiratory infections.

As far as other diseases are concerned, cases of kidney stones and arthritis deserve attention. Both of these conditions are found frequently among prisoners from concentration camps and have been regarded as consequences from the prisoner's lack of calcium in their diet while in the camps.

The Holocaust changed the face of the Jewish people. The large Jewish communities of Poland that were also centers of Torah study and Jewish thought are now gone forever. In 1900, eighty-one percent of all the Jews in the world lived in Europe. Today, only a few communities remain – the Jews have ceased to be a European people altogether.

It is said that the passage of time helps ease the pain and can help get rid of the grief over loss of relatives and community. It can also be said that time creates perspective and that would enable everyone to see the historic significance of the events.

For the Jewish people, the Holocaust is a lesson in history, which is a permanent part of their lives. The course of Jewish history has left Europe. The future lies in a contest between the American Jewish community and the Israeli Jewish community.

Wlodawa, Poland

Growing up, my father would tell me very few stories about his life before and during WWII. It was rare for parents to talk to their children about the appalling events that occurred leading up to and during the Holocaust. So, when he took the time to tell a story, I would be careful to take in each word. Every now and again my father would surprise us by recollecting, with a warm half smile, back to his childhood and take a minute or two to affectionately describe bits and pieces of happier times growing up on the large family farm where his parents bred and raised horses for the Polish military.

His parents had passed away due to various illnesses when my father was young. A possible scenario that has been discussed recently is that my grandfather mysteriously disappeared and could have died during a *pogrom* (a riot against Jews). As a result of these misfortunes, my father was now parentless and sent to live in an orphanage. He resided amongst other orphaned children with his younger brother and sister.

Although my father was in an orphanage with his younger siblings, he had older siblings that were able to work and fend for themselves. At that time they did not need to depend on the orphanage to care for them. One brother, Efraim, worked as a laborer.

Shortly after the Germans took over Wlodawa, they rounded up all the Jewish residents and forced them in to an appointed ghetto. This ghetto was located in the neighborhood of 1000-lecia, Błotna and Kotlarska Streets. In the ghetto, Nazis held not only the local Jewish population, but also Jews from Cracow, Mielec, and Vienna. It is there where my father ended up with the rest of his family forced to live, work, and begin their unjustified suffering.

From the spring of 1942, the numbers of the Jewish population in Wlodawa rose considerably because of the deportees from the German Reich. Conditions of life in the ghetto (to judge from the few eye witnesses' reports) were extremely difficult.

In the ghetto, for their own menacing entertainment, the Germans would spare no expense when it came to annihilating a person's will in order to humiliate and control their 'prisoners' for their own warped sense of humor. They carried this out regularly by securing men with lengths of tightly braided rope to heavily overloaded carts. This work used to be done with horses, but not anymore; the Germans had other inhumane plans for transporting the carts.

Randomly chosen Jew's were forcefully tied up to the carts to act as the "horse" and do the animal's job for them. Frightened and defenseless, they stood motionless just waiting to hear the German's bark out their next belittling order, which was to carry out the command given to them and hurriedly start pulling the cart.

As they began their almost impossible task, the Germans in numbers began to unmercifully beat the "puller" to the edge of unconsciousness and exhaustion. They would then expect these weakened, near death souls to continue pulling the heavy loads to a predetermined destination while the Germans followed closely; laughing and taunting their captives along the way.

One particular day, the Germans began their game of beating one of the cart pullers. Everyone was lined up in a steadfast formation along the street curb, eyes straight forward. It was mandatory that everyone bare witness to the day's "event".

As a few agonizing minutes of the beating took place, my father quickly (but cautiously) studied the face of the soon to be "puller" and realized the man he was staring at was his Uncle. As my father helplessly stood by wishing he could intervene, the Germans continued their relentless beating of his Uncle and persisted to show no mercy while seemingly taking pleasure in doing so. They eventually beat him to his undeserved death. My father absolutely could do nothing for him but pray that it would all be over soon. My father believed the Germans were making an example of him so that the others would continue to live in fear and never contemplate the thought of making things difficult by trying to escape the ghetto.

Prior to the beating of his uncle, my father's brother (Efraim) had told him that he was going to sneak out of the ghetto and leave for Russia. At the time my father asked him to take their younger brother and sister with him out of the ghetto, but Efraim said that they were too young and it was too risky for them. Their younger brother and sister would eventually be sent to the Sobibor extermination camp.

Recollecting the memory of his brother leaving for Russia was all my father could think about after the incident earlier in the day with his uncle. It was at this point he knew the ghetto had become much too dangerous for him to continue living in. On the day of his uncle's death, he decided he would sneak out of the ghetto that night and leave for Russia.

Jews put together for roll call.

Polish Army

When my father first arrived in Russia, he was fortunate enough to secure a job in a large factory. He was also lucky enough to find a non-Jewish family willing to rent a room to him, which he paid for with bread. In those days bread actually held more value as currency than money itself! He saved what little money he could and enrolled himself into night school. Around that time he started hearing about the on-going turmoil within the now unofficial German occupied Poland. Not wanting to escape to sit by idly in Russia while his family and people were being rounded up and innocently killed, my father learned that the Polish army was recruiting members in many different territories outside of Poland to fight alongside Russia for the cause.

My father made the only decision that he deemed justifiable, which was to join the Polish Army to fight in honor of his family and for his county's freedom. Although it might sound strange to join one countries military while in another, the Polish Army was actually being supported by Russia because Poland was invaded and subsequently taken over by Germany (although the Polish Government never officially surrendered to Germany).

While in the Polish military, my father was severely wounded fighting for the liberation of Poland. One day he would go on to tell me in detail just how the scenario unfolded:

"Our entire unit moved with skilled precision over the open terrain on our way back to Poland, some 50 yards ahead in the distance we all heard a large explosion, the first shell had landed, we were under attack! A thick black cloud of smoke could be seen billowing upward as a slight wind gusted and carried it away. Just then, another large explosion could be felt rumbling through the ground 50 yards behind us, which shook the soldiers in our command vehicle," he told me.

He felt that the next shell was bound to be a direct hit so the driver was ordered to turn off course to avoid taking fire. Just when he did, he accidentally steered the vehicle straight into a ditch. As they anxiously tried to get out, they were confronted with the realization they were now face to face with a German anti-tank gunner.

The gunner took advantage of their dilemma and was ready to score a direct hit. As the gunner began to fire on the vehicle, my father said he could vividly remember feeling a large concussion and hearing a severe high-pitched noise ringing in his ears. The taste of noxious fumes filled his mouth and started burning his now smoke filled lungs. At this point, he said he could barely breathe or see exactly what was going on around him. He was disoriented for what seemed an eternity but he gathered himself long enough to figure out that the vehicle was severely damaged and out of commission.

As the smoke dissipated, his eyes still burning and cloudy, he could make out that their officer was still alive but very badly hurt. Unfortunately, eight of the other soldiers in the convoy weren't so lucky, and died as a result of the attack. Once my father could properly assess the situation, he paced around angrily trying to decide what measure should be taken next.

As he contemplated what had just happened, my father could feel a sharp throbbing pain and a warm sensation moving down the length of his leg. He took a moment to look himself over and discovered he had taken shrapnel in his thigh and what he was actually feeling was the blood flowing right down his leg and straight into his boot.

He could faintly hear someone calling out his name, "Michal, Michal, Are you ok?" "No", he answered. "I am terribly in need of help."

The soldier yelled out for a medic. He came over with a stretcher and two men carried him to a field tent for medical assistance. A field surgeon came to examine my father's wound, which was pretty bad due to the extent of shrapnel that was lodged in his leg and advised that he would have to immediately remove as much of it as he could so that infection would not set in.

Three days later, my father was back marching into battle to liberate his homeland of Poland from the German stronghold. Unfortunately, with the circumstance of being treated in a "field hospital" they could not remove every piece of metal. The smaller bits of shrapnel would have to remain in my father's leg for the rest of his life, which caused him much pain and discomfort.

Once the war officially ended, my father made his way to Warsaw to register himself in Poland as a displaced person and to end his enlistment in the Polish military. He then spent his time traveling through Poland visiting a number of Kibbutz's looking for any possible surviving relatives. It was in one of the Kibbutz's where he would eventually meet my mother.

My mother recalls that a short time after meeting my father they happened to be walking through town when a high-ranking Officer approached and respectfully saluted my father. Only, my father did not salute back. She couldn't quite grasp the concept as to why the soldier took this position towards another military man. Being that my mother is so inquisitive, she decided to ask why he did not reciprocate with a salute back? He simply replied, "I am not an enlisted soldier in the military anymore." With a slightly puzzled look on my mother's face, my father went on to explain, "I can understand why the Officer saluted me, but, this uniform just happens to be the only clothes I own at the moment so I didn't feel it was necessary for me to return the gesture!"

Polish Military Tank

Sobibor

In 1942, Germans started to dissolve the Wlodawa ghetto successively by deporting its residents in a few transports to the Sobibor extermination camp and executing them afterwards.

Sobibor was the second of three extermination camps constructed to murder the population of adjacent ghettos and other victims of surrounding areas. Sobibor measured roughly 1,300 by 2,000 feet. The camp was surrounded by a triple line of barbed wire fencing, which was intertwined with pine branches to prevent observation from the outside (including the station area). Each corner of the camp was highly guarded by large wooden watchtowers.

Sobibor was located in the far east of Poland near the borders of the now modern states of Belarus and the Ukraine. The camp had to be located near main railway lines since victims were transported this way. They also had to be located in sparsely populated areas due the secret operation of the camp that was demanded. In mid-April 1942, when the camp was nearly completed, experimental gassings took place.

Erich Fuchs, who spent time at the three Reinhard death camps of Sobibor, Treblinka, and Bełżec, explained how the gassing operation at Sobibor began:

"Upon arriving in Sobibor, I discovered a piece of open ground close to the station on which there was a concrete building and several other permanent buildings. The Sonderkommando at Sobibor was led by Thomalla. Amongst the SS personnel there were Floss, Bauer, Stangl, Schwarz, Barbl and others.

We unloaded the motor. It was a heavy, Russian petrol engine (presumably a tank or tractor engine) of at least 200 HP (carburettor engine, eight-cylinder, water-cooled). We put the engine on a concrete plinth and attached a pipe to the exhaust outlet. Then we tried out the engine. At first it did not work. I repaired the ignition and the valve and suddenly the engine started.

The chemist whom I already knew from Belzec went into the gas chamber with a measuring device in order to measure the gas concentration.

After this, a test gassing was carried out. I seem to remember that thirty to forty women were gassed in a gas chamber. The Jewesses had to undress in a clearing in the wood, which had been roofed over, near the gas chamber. They were herded into the gas chamber like helpless animals being led to their slaughter by the above-mentioned SS members and Ukrainian volunteers.

When the women had been locked up in the gas chamber, I attended to the engine together with Bauer. The engine immediately started ticking over. We both stood next to the engine and switched it up to "release exhaust to chamber" so that the gases were channeled into the engine and switched it up to "release exhaust to chamber" so that the gases were channeled into the chamber. The chemist insisted that I rev up the engine, which meant that no extra gas had to be added later. After about ten minutes of gasping and painfully struggling for air, thirty to forty women were dead. The chemist and the SS gave the signal to turn off the engine.

I packed up my tools and saw the bodies being taken away. A small wagon on rails was used to take them away from near the gas chamber to a stretch of ground some distance away. Sobibor was the only place where a wagon was used. "

Roughly a month later, Sobibor became fully operational. The begginning of the mass gassing operation started. Trains entered the railway station daily. The Jews onboard were told they were in a transit camp, and were forced to undress and hand over their valuables. They were then led along the 100 meter long *Himmelstrasse* (road to heaven) which led to the gas chambers, where they were suffocated and subsequently killed.

Before the Jews undressed, *Oberscharführer* Hermann Michel made a speech to them. On these occasions, he used to wear a white "medical" coat to give the impression he was a physician. Michel announced to the Jews that they would be sent to work, but, before this they would have to take baths and undergo disinfection to prevent the spread of diseases.

After undressing, the Jews were taken through the tube, by an SS man leading the way, with five or six Ukrainians at the back hurrying the Jews along. After the Jews entered the gas chambers, the Ukrainians closed the doors. The motor was switched on by the former Soviet soldier Emil Kostenko and by the German driver Erich Bauer from Berlin. After the gassing, the doors were opened and the corpses were removed by a group of Jewish workers.

One source states that up to 200,000 people were killed at Sobibor. In the Hagen court proceedings against former Sobibor Nazis, Professor Wolfgang Scheffler, who served as an expert, estimated the total figure of murdered Jews at a minimum of 250,000. The reason that they were able to kill so quickly and efficienltly was due to the "improvements" they made in chamber capacity. The SS halted deportations for two months to Sobibor in order to "modernize" the railway system into the camp.

By reconstructing and adding new chambers during the two month lull in transports to Sobibor, it allowed camp authorities to kill up to 1,300 people at a time.

Furnace in a camps crematorium

Sobibor Uprising

During the Holocaust there were only two successful uprisings by Jewish prisoners in the extermination camps. One of these uprisings took place at Sobibor.

On October 14, 1943, members of the Sobibor underground, led by Polish-Jewish prisoner Leon Feldhendler and Soviet-Jewish POW Alexander Pechersky, succeeded in covertly killing eleven German SS officers and a number of camp guards. Although their plan was to kill all the SS and walk out of the main gate of the camp, the killings were discovered and the inmates ran for their lives under heavy gunfire. About 300 out of the 600 prisoners in the camp escaped into the forests.

However, only fifty to seventy escapees survived the war. Some died as a result of having the misfortune of stepping on land mines, which littered the fields surrounding the camp, and some were recaptured in a dragnet and executed by the Germans in the next few days. Most of those who did survive were hidden from the Germans by other Poles, at the risk of their own and their families' lives.

Within days after the uprising, the SS chief Heinrich Himmler ordered the camp closed, dismantled, and for trees to be planted on the grounds where the camp was previously - to hide evidence that it ever existed.

Passing The Torch

Intergenerational trauma is being passed along from immediate Holocaust survivors to their offspring. The trauma that is attributed to Holocaust-related influences can be seen in the children of Holocaust survivors, the background story tends to be either a stifled mystery or overflowing with upsetting information.

Holocaust survivors endured incredible humiliation and struggle for survival; there was starvation, violence, fear and horror during the war and then after being liberated they came to new countries to start over. The second-generation experienced a mix of shame for their parents' lacked language and social skills which was a bad combination mixed with the guilt over what the parents had endured.

The Holocaust is a crime that will never subside. Even as the ranks of survivors grow smaller each year, the impact of the history continues to be felt. It's not just the victims who feel the effects; it's their children, too.

According to studies, the long-term effects of the Holocaust on the children of survivors suggest a "psychological profile". Their parents' suffering may have affected their upbringing, personal relationships, and perspective on life. Other characteristics suggest affected identity, self-esteem, interpersonal interactions, and worldview.

Psychologists have long been intrigued by the emotional profile of so-called second-generation Holocaust survivors. Parents who lived through the camps were forever changed by the crimes committed against them. In the 21st century, many would be recognized as suffering from post-traumatic stress disorder (PTSD). Back then, the absence of such a diagnosis also meant the absence of effective treatments.

As a result, a generation of children grew up in homes in which one (and sometimes both) parents were battling untold emotional demons at the same time they were going about the difficult business of trying to raise happy kids.

It was no surprise that they weren't always entirely successful. Over the years, a large body of work has been devoted to studying PTSD symptoms in second-generation survivors, and it has found signs of the condition in their behavior and even their blood, with higher levels of the stress hormone cortisol, for example. The perfectly reasonable assumption was always that these symptoms were essentially learned.

If you were to grow up with parents afflicted with the mood swings, irritability, and jumpiness typical of PTSD, you're likely to wind up a bit stressed and somewhat high strung yourself.

This legacy can be a burden or a gift. For those who have accepted this important legacy, you are not alone. Your feelings are shared by countless others. The Jewish people have worked diligently to make sure that their children do not forget the tragedies of the Holocaust.

There is no yardstick for personal suffering; personal misery and sorrow cannot be measured, nor should it be denied.

To some second-generation children, they see this legacy as a gift. For those who accept the legacy of the Holocaust as a gift, I insist that you respect this dignified honor. Keep in mind, it is a vital part of your history too. Do not let anyone deny that your parents, your grandparents, or anyone in your family for that matter suffered dearly during those tumultuous years. Remember, they were incarcerated against their will, tortured, enslaved, and murdered in inexcusable numbers.

Some of our parents and grandparents rose up and fought valiantly with homemade weapons to protect themselves and their homeland. I cannot express how important this part of our history is to embrace. Having respect and admiration for those who suffered in the past will positively affect our future for generations to come. Do this, not only to honor our forefathers, but also for your children's sake - as one day it will be their torch to carry forward.

Holocaust Denial

Holocaust denial is the belief that during WWII Jews were not murdered on as much of a mass scale (5-6 million killed) as history states. Holocaust deniers also claim that Germans did not use gas chambers or extermination camps to kill Jews, and that there was no official policy to the murders of the Jewish people. Holocaust deniers also claim that many of the photos and documents from the Holocaust are fabricated, and were used by the Allies to make the Germans, who obviously lost the war, look more evil then they ever actually were.

Many of the deniers state that the Holocaust is just a story created by Jewish people to further a "Jewish Conspiracy" at the expense of others. For this reason, and because Holocaust denial is usually preconceived long before looking at any facts, denial of the Holocaust is not considered just a corrupt form of 'revisionism', but also considered anti-semetic.

Holocaust deniers do not like to be called "deniers", but instead "revisionists". A "revisionist" is a term that can be used by credible historians who question events that have happened in the past, in order to look at them from a different angle for a better understanding since "lions write history".

The major difference between the deniers and the actual history revisionists is that Holocaust denier's selectively leave out major facts to back up their theories. There are also many cases where Holocaust deniers have modified images professionally and used known fake documents as references for their speeches and books. Because of this, it is inappropriate to call a Holocaust denier anything but that, because there is a lack of credibility that would be given to any other historical researcher.

A couple of the points that deniers use to back up their beliefs are that survivors stories are inconsistent and filled with errors, and this makes them unreliable sources. Another is that there is no mass scale of paperwork or evidence that shows that the Germans had a specific plan to intentionally kill off the Jewish race.

If there is an inconsistency in a survivor's story, it is because most survivors went many decades after the Holocaust without wanting to remember or even think about the atrocities that were done to them. Many of the survivors were also young children at the time, faced with extreme stress on their body and minds because of the hard labor and death of many close relatives. To attack a Holocaust survivor because in their old age they have to try hard to remember memories from when they were young and faced with extreme pain (that they spent their entire life trying to forget) is not only wrong, but also inhumane and inappropriate.

When it comes to missing documents, there is no surprise that it is hard to find evidence of the genocide of the Jewish people. As the Germans were facing the reality that they were possibly going to lose the war, they began to order the disposal of the incriminating evidence of what they had been doing to the unfortunate people murdered while imprisoned in the camps. This was done because the Germans knew that there was a possibility that they would have to face trial after the war.

Heinrich Himmler had given orders to Nazi's for the destruction of papers, bodies, and the gas chambers to try and have any and all evidence disappear.

During this time, there are also many examples of Nazi's digging up mass graves that were created a couple years prior, and the thousands of human remains set on fire to try and cover up any possible negative fallout if found. Germans were afraid that surviving Jews would give testimony and lead Allied Forces to the mass graves and dig them up as evidence.

Holocaust deniers are some of the most offensive people that the Jewish community has to deal with when it comes to remembering the victims of the Holocaust. Holocaust denial is a growing problem and continues to be a negative force as anti-semetic and anti-israel groups and countries try to rewrite history because of their own hatred for Israel or the Jewish people.

As a people, we will continue to move forward in our lives and history, and fight the negative and uncalled for racial hatred that is pointed at us. We will always remember our struggles and our many accomplishments, even with the copious odds against us.

We have succeeded in the past five thousand years, and we will continue to succeed no matter what obstacles are placed in front of us.

My father (bottom row, 4th from right)
and siblings in Orphanage

מדינה ישראל

משרד העליה

המ׳ לבקרת הגבולות

תחנת הבקרת בנמל ___מ_פ_ק_ח___   (ל)

בשדה תעופה ___נמל חיפה___

תעודת רישום

התעודה הזאת נתנה לאשור שה׳ ___אקר מוסק אלינטר___

שם אשתו ___נילי___

שמות הילדים _____

___אלינטר___

הורענו) ..דינת ישראל ביום

באניה/באוירון ___5/5/47___ ונרשם(ת)

א) כעולה(ים) לפי מספר ___128187___

ב) כחוזר(ת) (ים)

ג) כתייר(ת) (ים)

תאריך ___JULY 1949___

קצין בקרת הגבול

1003/V,49/15,000   טופס על/11

RZECZPOSPOLITA POLSKA

Województwo lubelskie

Urząd Stanu Cywilnego w Włodawie

Nr 357/1933/Mż   Włodawa, lata 18 sierpnia 1933 r.

ODPIS ZUPEŁNY AKTU URODZENIA

I. Dane dotyczące dziecka:

1. Nazwisko Ekhauz

2. Imię (imiona) Mordechaj

3. Płeć męska

4. Data urodzenia siódmego września tysiąc dziewięćset dwudziestego drugiego (07.09.1922) roku (godz. 22:00)

5. Miejsce urodzenia Włodawa

II. Dane dotyczące rodziców:

	Ojciec	Matka
1. Nazwisko	Ekhauz	Ekhauz
2. Imię (imiona)	Lejzor Josel	Cyrla
3. Nazwisko rodowe	Ekhauz	Buchbinder
4. Data urodzenia	lat 44	
5. Miejsce urodzenia		
6. Miejsce zamieszkania w chwili urodzenia dziecka	Włodawa	

III. Dane dotyczące osoby (zakładu) zgłaszającej urodzenie:

1. Nazwisko i imię (nazwa zakładu) .....Ekhauz Lejzor Josel~~~~~~~~~

2. Miejsce zamieszkania (siedziba zakładu) Włodawa~~~~~~~~~~~~~~~~~~

IV. Uwagi: ...Dziecko zostało uznane przez ojca Ekhauza
~~Lejzora w dniu dzisiejszym.~~~~~~~~~~~~~~~~~~~~~~~~~

Podpis osoby zgłaszającej

/-/ Ekhauz Lejzor Josel
KIEROWNIK
Urzędu Stanu Cywilnego

/-/ podpis nieczytelny

Wzmianki dodatkowe: ....

Opłatę skarbową w
wysokości 33 zł.
uiszczono dnia;
2010-11-2B Nr
konta: 36 1240 2249
1111 0010 2099 3235

Poświadcza się zgodność powyższego odpisu
z treścią aktu w księdze urodzeń.

Włodawa data ...03.11.2010......
KIEROWNIK
Urzędu Stanu Cywilnego

M-4 „DRUK-HURT", Łódź (0-42) 682-24-11

A list of Eckhaus's from the Wlodawa Orphanage and
School (obtained through research - Polish/Wlodawa government)

My Father

ECKHAUS Rywka Bejla   (b. 07.02.1923) Wlodawa   [class 1c, 2c, 3c - 1930-1934]

        Motel   (b. 15.08.1923) - Cyrla-mother   [class 2a, 3a, 3c - 1931-1934]

        Etla   (b. 1919) Wlodawa   [class 1d - 1926-1927]

        Rywka   (b. 29.01.1923) Wlodawa   [class 1c - 1931-1932]

        Izaak (Icchak) (b.18.11.1920) Wlodawa   [class 2b,3b,4b,4c - 1929-1934]

        Dawid   (b.1919) Wlodawa   [class 1e - 1926-1927]

        Roza   (b.1918) Wlodawa   [class 5b - 1932-1933]

        Fuma   (b.14.09.1915) Wlodawa   [class 3a - 1926-1927]

        Dawid   (b.07.10.1918) Wlodawa   [class 2c, 3c - 1930-1933]

        Roza   (b. 1917) Wlodawa   [class 1d - 1926-1927]

        Froim   (b. 26.12.1917) Wlodawa   [class 2b - 1929-1930]

        Abram   (b. 15.05.1923) Wlodawa   [class 1c, 2d, 2a, 3a]

and: Fejga Chuma (b. 23.05.1927), Pinchos - Motel (b. 01.05.1927), Zelman (b. 15.09.1929), Deworc (b. 28.01.1926),
Masza (b. 1926), Mirla (b. 22.07.1931), Jakiw Jochalz (b. 27.12.1929), Frejda (b.13.01.1931),
Jakiw Icchak (b. 27.12.1929).

the names of the Eckhaus's in the orphanage: Mordehaj (age: 12) - from 1933 to 1939

                                                Jankiel (age: 7) - from 1937 to 1939

The Great Synagogue (Wlodawa)